Pebble® Plus

Helping the Environment

I Can Reuse and Recycle

by Mary Boone

CAPSTONE PRESS
a capstone imprint

Pebble Plus is published by Pebble
1710 Roe Crest Drive, North Mankato, Minnesota 56003
www.mycapstone.com

Library of Congress Cataloging-in-Publication Data
Library of Congress Cataloging-in-Publication Data is
available on the Library of Congress website.
ISBN 978-1-9771-0310-9 (library binding)
ISBN 978-1-9771-0520-2 (paperback)
ISBN 978-1-9771-0318-5 (eBook PDF)

Editorial Credits
Anna Butzer, editor; Kayla Rossow, designer;
Tracy Cummins, media researcher; Kathy McColley, production specialist

Image Credits
Capstone Studio: Karon Dubke, 11; Getty Images: Tim Pannell/Corbis/VCG, Cover;
iStockphoto: FangXiaNuo, 17, martinedoucet, 13, Paul Bradbury, 9, Steve Debenport, 19;
Shutterstock: Arina P Habich, 15, Blend Images, 7, Cultura Motion, 21, Kumer Oksana,
Back Cover, Ms Moloko, Design Element, vchal, 5

Note to Parents and Teachers

The Helping the Environment set supports national curriculum standards for science
and community. This book describes and illustrates reusing and recycling. The images
support early readers in understanding the text. The repetition of words and phrases helps
early readers learn new words. This book also introduces early readers to subject-specific
vocabulary words, which are defined in the Glossary section. Early readers may need
assistance to read some words and to use the Table of Contents, Glossary, Read More,
Internet Sites, CriticalThinking Questions, and Index sections of the book.

Printed in the United States   5050

Table of Contents

Too Much Trash!

Look at all the trash in that landfill! It rots and gives off gases that pollute the air. Yuck! Recycling and reusing cut down on waste.

Want to help save the environment? We can if we reuse and recycle. I can reuse old items. I find new ways to use them.

Small Changes for Reusing

Our family finds things that can be reused. I bring cloth bags to the grocery store. We avoid using plastic bags.

I see an empty soup can.
It can hold my markers and
colored pencils. I decorate it
to make it look nice.

I bring my own lunch to school. I pack it in a reusable lunch box. We are careful to avoid plastic bags that can only be used one time.

My family does not throw away empty milk gallon jugs. They are cleaned and used again. We use them as planters or watering cans.

Recycling Makes a Difference!

My family sorts bottles and cans. We sort cardboard and paper too. All of these items can be recycled. We place them in special bins.

At school, we look for ways we can reuse and recycle. Together we plan a clothing drive. We collect used clothing for people in need.

When we reuse and recycle, we are helping to save the environment. Together we can all make the world a healthy and safe place to live.

Glossary

environment—the natural world of the land, water, and air

drive—an organized project to do something

gas—a form of matter that is not solid or liquid; it can move about freely and does not have a definite shape

healthy—fit and well, not sick

landfill—a system of trash and garbage disposal in which the waste is buried between layers of earth

pollute—to make something dirty or unsafe

recycle—to make used items into new products; people can recycle items such as rubber, glass, plastic, and aluminum

Read More

Lindeen, Mary. *Reduce, Reuse, Recycle.* A Beginning to ReadBook. Chicago: Norwood House Press, 2018

Paul, Miranda, and Elizabeth Zunon. *One Plastic Bag: Isatou Ceesay and the Recycling Women of the Gambia.* Millbrook Press, 2015.

Pettiford, Rebecca. *Recycling.* Green Planet Minneapolis: Pogo, 2017

Internet Sites

FactHound offers a safe, fun way to find Internet sites related to this book. All of the sites on FactHound have been researched by our staff.

Here's all you do:

Visit *www.facthound.com*

Type in this code: 9781977103109

Super-cool stuff! Check out projects, games and lots more at **www.capstonekids.com**

Critical Thinking Questions

1. Can you think of ways to reuse old worksheets or notepaper?

2. What are ways that your class or school could reduce waste?

3. What steps could you take to make it easier to recycle at home?

Index